Library of Congress Cataloging-in-Publication Data:

Names: Chronicle Books (Firm), compiler.
Title: Cute animals for hard times / [compilation by] Chronicle Books LLC.
Description: San Francisco : Chronicle Books, [2020]
Identifiers: LCCN 2020009516 | ISBN 9781797203317 (hardback)
Subjects: LCSH: Animals--Pictorial works. | Animals--Humor.
Classification: LCC QL46 .C48 2020 | DDC 590.22/2--dc23
LC record available at https://lccn.loc.gov/2020009516

Manufactured in China.

MIX
Paper from
responsible sources
FSC
www.fsc.org   FSC™ C104723

Design by Evelyn Furuta.

10 9 8 7 6 5 4 3 2

Chronicle books and gifts are available at special quantity discounts
to corporations, professional associations, literacy programs, and
other organizations. For details and discount information,
please contact our corporate/premiums department at
corporatesales@chroniclebooks.com or at 1-800-759-0190.

Chronicle Books LLC
680 Second Street
San Francisco, California 94107
www.chroniclebooks.com

CUTE ANIMALS
FOR HARD TIMES

CHRONICLE BOOKS

SAN FRANCISCO

BUTTERFLY BOOPS